THE WONDER OF LOVE

Edited by

Heather Killingray

First published in Great Britain in 2004 by
POETRY NOW
Remus House,
Coltsfoot Drive,
Peterborough, PE2 9JX
Telephone (01733) 898101
Fax (01733) 313524

SB ISBN 1 84460 808 5

FOREWORD

Although we are a nation of poets we are accused of not reading poetry, or buying poetry books. After many years of listening to the incessant gripes of poetry publishers, I can only assume that the books they publish, in general, are books that most people do not want to read.

Poetry should not be obscure, introverted, and as cryptic as a crossword puzzle: it is the poet's duty to reach out and embrace the world.

The world owes the poet nothing and we should not be expected to dig and delve into a rambling discourse searching for some inner meaning.

The reason we write poetry (and almost all of us do) is because we want to communicate: an ideal; an idea; or a specific feeling. Poetry is as essential in communication, as a letter; a radio; a telephone, and the main criterion for selecting the poems in this anthology is very simple: they communicate.

CONTENTS

SOMETIMES I LAY WITH YOU AT NIGHT

Sometimes I lay with you at night
And there's not a single sound.
Those times when I'm close to you
My thoughts become a line –
And I don't know if the heart I hear
Is your heart beating, or mine.

Pablo Rose

BRIEF ENCOUNTER

I wondered what her name was?
The girl I saw that day
Stood between her parents
All packed and going away
A suitcase and a shoulder bag
Stood on the platform row
And as she leant to pick them up
She turned and smiled: 'Hello.'

I wondered where she came from?
That girl on platform three
I still remember well her eyes
The same she turned to me
As green as grass, soft emeralds
Un-minéd gems so pure
They were the most enchanting eyes
My young eyes ever saw.

I wondered where it was she went
When she boarded on the train?
As I stood a moment longer I
Still blushing on her name
As those eyes began to pull away
And leave with me my sigh
A lasting picture frames my mind
She turned and smiled: 'Goodbye . . . '

I wonder if she ever knew
She took away my breath
The same that breathed the life in me
That froze young love bereft
For now an old man sits a chair
Content . . . but stirs a thought
For a young girl once a young man loved
But fate said no . . . that's all . . .

M J Banasko

LONGING

I long for your love in the heat of the night
I seek reassurance instead of the fight
with misunderstandings and tears brought about
by deep insecurity, fault finding, doubt!

We ought to have dealt with these problems before.
When seeds sown in anger just harvested more;
when we didn't talk as the issues arose
and mountains from molehills grew huge I suppose.

It's all in the past now and so hard to deal
with the hurt and painful confusion we feel.
The reasons we loved in the first place are lost
and saying 'I'm sorry' is too high a cost.

I long for those days at the birth of this love!
Excitement at seeing you, all I dreamed of.
But now when we meet, complications take hold,
the warmth of our love has grown stale, become cold.

Please hold me, make love to me, shed your thick skin,
let me see, once again, the real you that's within.
This armour we wear causes nothing but pain,
be naked with me, help me find 'us' again.

Ali Paterson

HER WORD

You copy and paste your laughter
Into the document of my day
And I save as
To a thousand different places,

A myriad of different formats
Zipped and unzipped . . .

Kate Symons

I NEVER KNEW
(For MJB)

I never knew what love was
Until the day that I found you
Never knew what it meant
To be the other half
Of a perfect whole
Never knew that thoughts,
Dreams, desires
Could be shared so completely
Never knew what it was
To live
To awaken at another's touch
Until the day that I found you.

Helen Ambler

VOW TO MY SOULMATE

'I'm nothing special,' you once said
If so, I'm nothing special too
But you were the one that believed in me
And so I write these words for you

I don't need a church
On some sunny day in June
Don't need to exchange bands of gold
Or walk to a wedding tune

Don't need to look like a fluffy meringue
Or stand before a god to approve
Don't need to sign bits of paper
To spend my life loving you

You don't even need to be near me
Or speak to me ever again
And I don't need your permission
To be in love with you 'til the end

But I would never try to own you
Try to entrap you or possess
All I ask is that one day
You might end my emptiness

And so from this day forward
My heart will be faithful to you
I give you my dreams, hold them close
I know they're your dreams too

Carol Wheeler

DIFFERENT

It's strange why we love one another,
When we're so different in every way,
I always chatter endlessly,
While you carefully choose each word you say.

I could listen to a song forever,
You stride into the room and turn off my CD,
Then you study the financial pages of The Times,
I'm content to read some poetry.

It's sad I'm a muddle of emotions,
Watching waves of logic surf your level head,
Sometimes I lie awake worrying,
You sleep the minute after sinking into bed.

I see you with a bar of chocolate,
You're happy with a piece or two,
How can you manage not to eat the lot?
Many a time I wish I knew.

It's strange why we love one another,
When so often we seem poles apart,
But there is no sense or reason,
When it comes to feelings of the heart.

Elaine Beresford

SILENT HEART

When a marriage
Is sown together with true love
No matter how hard sometimes
You pull at the seam
The stitches will
Always remain
Intact

Lisa Killeen

2739 ELLSWORTH

Harsh words are heard between
two lovers next door
each bearing shields of mistrust
and pride that cover only
I love you.

Their door slowly opens
and her crying issues forth
upon a doyen near
a memory fresh and clear
of words he never spoke
I love you.

James Rasmusson

MY VALENTINE

I'm living again the world's such a treat,
and a gossamer image has made a repeat.
This time it's for certain not just in my dreams,
whatever happens, it's a little surreal.
The sun kisses the mountain exposed to its rays,
my heart beats to a rhythm like the ripples of waves.
My Valentine hero now controlling my thoughts,
leading me forward to greet a new dawn.
What lies in the future? I really can't tell,
when you've met your heart throb and your world starts anew,
let's leave tomorrow and what continues to be,
surprises untold for our future to be.
Evenings grow lighter, darkness ceases to be,
the sun gives its power to nature and me.
I'm happy, I'm carefree completely at ease,
having now met my true love; well my life is a breeze.

J Prentice

AMERICAN LOVE

Why do I love Whitman?
For his grabbing of big spaces.
The way he paints a detailed picture
of stones, drums and birds.
The song of himself.

But this is not how
you love me.
You unpioneer my crevices,
make adventure out of dry
until it's wet.

Banish all airs and graces
with refinement of attention.
I am the one with all the ohs
not you. Exclamation is in my throat
an arch of such sheer lust I

lose discrimination.
Doggerel, give me
Betjeman at his worst.
I'll take kissograms,
verse on Valentine's cards,
hosts of golden daffodils, *ah*
but I want the way you do your short vowels in my ear.

Take Walt
and shuv 'im.

AnnMarie Eldon

ALLUSION

Mahler's fifth Symphony
unloosens barriers,
kindly mocks
forlorn façade.
It unlocks
passion's princely portals,
unleashes le soleil,
makes real, charade,
invites your love.

An interesting sky
daubed nectarine by nymphs
elusive,
lets its paint run,
intrusive,
shocks inertia to rose;
bracelets of light smile
second to none,
suggest we kiss.

Coppelia ballet
tranquillises the pain
of l'amour,
honies my heart,
subtle cure
for the torture of doubt;
pas de deux and I gasp.
shall you impart
that you love me?

Ruth Daviat

I MISS YOU

When I think of you,
It's with laughter never sadness, only joy,
When I hear you,
You awaken me; stir my passions and my thoughts.
When I speak to you,
It's with interest that I listen to what you say.
When I see you,
It's with pleasure as you brighten up my day.
When I miss you,
I miss your tenderness,
I miss the smile upon your face, your soft and gentle kisses,
And the warmth when we embrace.

Janet Evans

RHYMING COUPLETS

Often as you soften dreamily beside me
I hold an entire conversation with the
Pianissimo yet baroque harmonising;
Lulling the night airs with hot curled tongues chanting.
I speak of dreams, you pro-offer bounce and bounty,
I speak of dreads, you pervade a gentle beauty.

Often as you wriggle for a cosier pose
I ache for your sleepy dust sprinkled rose;
You pleasure between innocence and fantasy
Where flesh meets virgin's fear in grasped, panting cries.
My sense wander familiar garden paths
Bathing with my lover in sun drenched laughter,

And pasture in vivid texture musky kingdoms
Enjoying, undistractedly, rippled blossoms.
Often as you shift and shuffle, my head between
My forty something smile and my eager nineteen
Year old winks. So, what would you give? Not twenty years
I want to be the man of a thousand miles.

Often as you roll in sleep, I see the infant;
Even in cloudy mystery you eternalise the instant.
Often as you dream the iris bud flashes life,
A canvas of hues where passion intensifies,
Satisfies blooded interests and solaces.
An eternalised instant, earthly in lbliss.

Ian Lowery

A BRAND NEW DAWN
(For Rob and Charlotte)

From the dark nights of winter
Comes the freshness of a new year's spring,
Laying to rest the ghosts of the past
By seeing the future as clear as a mountain stream.
With the love that was lost, another has been found
A love so strong and giving
It's now time to walk your sacred ground.

An angel's watch will guide you as you walk along life's path
Sometimes it may be tender to the touch,
But most of all, being filled with a joy meant to last.
Looking upon your loved ones, as they watch over you
Believing in yourselves
Your lives will be a fairy tale come true.
With the love you share, the world is at your door,
You can change the greyest sky to blue
While watching as less people are announced poor.

Looking over your young ones
And nurturing the love from within,
The strength you carry will crumble mountains
And rid the world of sin.
By swimming the deepest ocean,
By catching a tear as it falls,
By walking the longest road
Your dreams may just turn to gold.

Looking back on what you've come through,
Knowing that you have weathered the storm,
Holding each other hand in hand, this is a new beginning
For this is the waking of a brand new dawn.

Richard Michael Grew

PATRICIA

We see the same moon,
Yet we cannot touch,
We live under the same stars,
Yet we cannot kiss,
Again you appeared in my dreams,
In a hazy room full of unknown people,
Your beautiful eyes stared all knowingly,
Your smile captivated my heart,
Someone said, 'Look behind you, Patricia is in.'
It took me a while; my pulse was racing,
Then I approached you and sat down,
Your hair was still long with golden streaks,
You always reminded me of the girl in 'Jean De Florette',
Or was it 'Manon des sources'? I don't know it was so long ago,
You spoke with that distinct smile,
Like in all dreams I sadly awoke feeling a strange warm emptiness,
The ghost of my loneliness had unlocked nostalgic memories,
                                        and left me wanting more,
Five years have passed since I saw you last,
Ten years have gone since I lost you,
I know you have a life now in France, where someone else has you
                                        for real every day,
I have someone too,
But occasionally Patricia you haunt me, you are very real in my heart
                                        and mind,
You come to me in my sleep,
A testimony to first love in spirit and in soul,
One that never dies,
I repeat again the last words I said to you,
'If I can't have you in this life, I'll wait for you at the gates of eternity.'
And to this I pledge my infinite love for you,
Patricia,
My Patricia.

Jon Aldersea

AH WELL!

I wonder, would I like to be
My lusty tomcat?
He
Who, never has to use his wiles
To gain a night out on the tiles,
Who fights off threats with tooth and claw
And rips out chunks of flesh and fur
From all the local opposition,
Confirming his top cat position;
He
Who, woos and wins vociferously,
Makes passionate love diurnally;
He
Who, never fails to pull
Besotted ladies by his call -
This peripatetic Romeo
With umpteen Juliets on the go;
He
Who, loves the livelong night,
Returns to bed at early light
Unreprimanded, sleeps all day
Then again begins his round of play.
I wonder . . .
Would I like to be
My lusty tomcat?
Me,
I'd give it a go -
The sexual athlete of Pimlico,
The Valentine of one and all
With an irresistible mating call
What could be wrong with that?

Ah well!

G Howarth

SWEET VALENTINE

Found in a box, a Valentine
With blood-red heart
Pierced by Cupid's arrow.
A pledge of true love
Forever; until
She with the angel-blue eyes
And cherry-ripe lips,
Stole you away from me.
What chance had I
To hold your heart,
So plain a Jane compared with
That Barbie doll temptress?
My sweet fickle-hearted Valentine
Where are you now?

Emelie Buckner

THE PERFECT VALENTINE

It came to me on St Valentine's Day
In an envelope with a heart
On the front and my name
Written in red ink!
I had other cards to read
But somehow this envelope and card
Intrigued me!
I opened the envelope
The card looked inviting
I opened it and out fell a photograph
The male face enthralled me
And written in red ink
I read;
'My name is Alex and I dearly love you'
The card had a verse in it;
'You are my heart's desire
Oh! How I would long to inspire
You and show my love
You, darling white innocent dove'
Alex; I wonder who you are?
Perhaps one day you will be my glowing star?
I do believe you are my perfect Valentine.

Alma Montgomery Frank

THE LETTERS

Dearest Love,

When last I put my pen to pad a healthy fire was glowing in the hearth,
the lake outside was frozen solid,
goodness, that seems along, long time ago.

It was January then, I remember, the sky was bleak
threatening any moment a fall of snow,
all the windowpanes were fern'd into beautiful patterns
large leaves and shapes were painted by the ice or frost.

Christmas had not very long been gone and
my only thoughts were, as always, yours and true, and
I still try to express what my heart wants to say
as, once again, I write to you.

The garden is now graced with two lovely white swans:
obviously lovers and quite new to our lake,
lots of dragonflies are hovering over the reed beds and lilies
and the frogs are croaking all day long.

It's now summer, of course, and the heat is fierce:
so much so I stay out of the sun;
I suppose, the next time I write it will be winter again
and another year will have come and gone.

Ever will you be close to my heart, and my thoughts of you
will go on and on.
I love the long letters you write to me
I do treasure them so every autumn and spring.

Well, I suppose I must close now; more I seem unable to write, and
I scarcely can think of any more I could say,
I rarely go out now, my limbs will not function,
but such pleasure I feel at any contact with you.

Do please take care.
You know I shall, as always, look forward to your next letter,
until then, all my love, as ever,
Violet, xxx.

Diana Mudd

WITHIN MY HEART

Within my heart you have a place,
A special place only I can see.
I have hidden my love, my fantasies.
On days when I look at you, I let them run free.
I watch as my love and fantasies unfold.
I want you and need you, and the love that flows.
Hold onto my heart my love, help to set me free.
The fantasies within my heart only you can set free.
Your touches, your hugs, are what my heart desires.
Fondle my heart let my desires run free.
Teach me to express my feelings.
Caress this body that so desires your touch.
Within my heart you have a place,
A special place that only you can enter.
Releasing my love, and fantasies.
That only you will see.
Holding you close, and stroking your body,
My fantasies unfold.
You are what my heart and soul desires.
You have a special place within my heart.

Jo Lodge

VALENTINE

From early days we two became good friends,
We were each of us seven years,
We'd share our scooters and whips and tops,
And play 'ticky' with our peers.
In summer we'd dabble in water clear
Making waterfalls in the stream;
Little touched by the World War holocaust,
It seems like a happy dream.
We'd go 'to tea' in each other's house,
No fussing on what we ate,
And Margaret would share our play
At the early age of eight!
Grown-ups would call us sweethearts
But I thought that was sloppy talk,
We'd parties enjoy with girls and boys
Or go for some rambling walk.
Our ways grew apart from early 'teens
And many years passed by,
But perhaps it's strange, though we'd many friends,
We're unmarried, he and I.
Some eighty years on we're both alive
And I don't think we repine;
Though we live far apart we are still in touch -
Would you call him my Valentine?

Kathleen M Hatton

THE MAN!

There is something about the man
An effervescence, look in his eyes
Which goes far beyond that of other men
There is something about the man
His heart reaches my heart
And touches my heart, so very sweetly
Yet overwhelmingly, with passion
I waited so long, look in his eyes
His kiss is pure sunshine
With the accent on pure
Swansdown to the touch, ethereal
His smile has a brimming jollity
And courage, a strength
There is something about the man
A lightness and a floating quality
Of other-worldliness, I waited so long
There is something about the man
Who is an enchanter, free of care
Free as air, look in his eyes
Of course I love the man, I love him to bits
I waited so long, for this day
He won my heart and took it away
And I took his, suddenly, in springtime
I needed it and wanted it
I desired his heart, his love, whatever it was
There is something about the man
I will always love him, I waited so long
Of course I love the man, I love him to bits
I will always love him, look in his eyes
He flies to my side and fills my being with delight
There is something about the man
A brimming effervescence, I waited so long

Margaret Bennett

SATURDAY 14TH FEBRUARY

What is this mass hysteria
Of pink ribbons and red hearts
Sickening chocolate 'I Love Yous'
In big padded cards?
What is this February 14th
This Valentine's Day?
A verse just for Grandma
There's no more to say

Andrew Allport

A POEM

I have a poem ringing in my ears
of the stormy seas and winds that sway
my heart's desire into far flung space -
the infinity of thoughts alas no more;
yet I had it loud, I had it clear - in dreams
that were no dreams, hallucinations that
were responding to my own will - creative
whenever I so wished.

For I am creation, created, creating -
yet the molten lava with cruel streaks of fire
flail the void in my soul when you
                        are not there;
                and emptiness shall reign
                and strings shall be broken
                and violins will into emptiness
                their dullness proclaim,
                with hollow sounds
                reverberating through ages
                        when you are not there
whenever I wished you to be here!

For I was creation, created, creating -
in a mirror of your thoughts as a frozen dream;
and when our cyclical time was ended
we still floated frozen on parallel courses
into eternity;
                as if you were not there,
                in those subjective dreams
                that perhaps hallucinations were -
yet always sweet 'though a raging sea
beat our craft
for admit,
                I was a good helmsman,
                one day off St Raphael.

J S Dembinski

HOLIDAY ROMANCE

In Tunisia.
We'd just been there on holiday.
We'd had a wonderful time sunning ourselves
On the beach in the resort of Sousse.
But now we were back home and back to reality.
I met him in a nightclub . . . the first night there.
We're in love . . . I rolled my eyes, for hours with him.
It's just a holiday romance, but in love . . . I said.
It's a both way thing; before I knew it, a tall, good-looking young man
Was standing on my doorstep . . . out of the blue.
'Hello, Mrs Carroll,' he said.
'It's an honour to meet you.'
I wanted to know what this man wanted from Lisa.
So deep inside, I had my suspicions.
He was polite and very loving towards Lisa.
She and Nader set up home in Rifle Street.
Through many months together; Lisa fell pregnant.
'We're getting married next week, Mum,' she said.
I was stunned . . . and sad by this answer.
'What's the rush?' I asked her.
'Wait until the baby comes and then we can have a proper job.'
She said, 'We've got to get married so Nader can get a visa
And stay in Britain, as he loves me so much.'
'I knew it,' I said.
I knew that's what he was after . . . all along.
On her wedding day I asked Lisa,
'Are you sure you're doing the right thing?'
'We're in love, we were going to get married anyway,' Lisa said.
'We're 100% sure we're in love, we're just bringing it forward.
I love him Mum, I'm so happy with him,' she said.
Three months later Lisa gave birth to a son.
They named him Hamza after Nader's little brother.
She was 19 years old. Nader was 24 years old.
Are they, convinced they found true love?

Viv Lionel Borer

GREEN EYES

I am consumed,
I am embraced,
I am secure
In his arms.

I am amazed,
I am assured,
I am saved
By his love.

I am there,
I am beautiful,
I am wanted
In his heart.

I am loved,
I am precious,
I am true,
I am lost
In his green eyes.

Becca Smith

VALENTINE ROSE

Red is the rose
That blows in the wind
Like the love of my life
Who beckons to me
Love is the whisper
That blows in the wind
Rose petals at my feet
Heady is the scent
Of the love of my life
A magical moment in my life
Blows Heaven's breath
Basking together
On a carpet of petals
We are together at last.

Patricia Turner

RAB WOULD TURN

Be ma darlin'
Kick yer heels
Spin ma wheels
Play for thrills.

How's about it babe?

Dawn Sansum

CELEBRATION OF LOVE

I come to celebrate
the love we share.
You are the glove
that fits my hand,
now and for all time.

We've got all the time in the world
as God's plan for us is revealed.
Ours is such a special love,
one that cannot be destroyed.

When I think of you
I am filled with joy.
You brought joy back into my life
when I was feeling low.

I love you so,
please don't go.
Stay here by my side,
be mine forever, Valentine!

Cathy Mearman

VALENTINE

One day is not enough
To express my love for you
I think I'll need a lifetime
And even that won't do

Endless as all time
As vast as the sea
How can I, in just one day
Show what you mean to me?

Romance and roses are the norm
The things that lovers share
But my valentine for you this year
Is my soul which I shall bare

Because today is what it is
My heart to you I'll give
But I'll give it to you willingly
Each day that I shall live.

Alex McKay

VALENTINE VERSE

I awoke one morning
On a sunny day
And gazed upon your sweet face.
The sunlight shining through the window
Left a trace
Of loving memories
Past and present.
The peaches and creams
And loves young dreams
You looked so lovely
Lying there
Your skin so pure
And your shoulders bare.
I love you with all my heart
I hope we will never part
Growing old together
And walk through
Fields of flowers,
My memories
'Will always be ours'.

Mary Woolvin

A Valentine For My Older Lover Who's Slow And Divine: Tantalising Me Sweetly And Sublime
(A spring and autumn romance of that very special kind)

Young womanhood bursting forth like the first flowers in early spring;
Jackie was a lovely girl who had all the young guys' hearts in a spin;
At just eighteen she had everything going for her in every way
But what the young roaring guys didn't know
Was that her sweet affections had turned another autumnal way!
'I know I call you my sugar daddy, because I'm just eighteen
And you are all of sixty-three:
But my sugar daddy Johnnie, I will always love you sweetly
Because you know the all romantic love woman in me:
And as I'm into the latest daring baring girly fashion thrills,
You sweetly pay for all my sexy fashion frills.
I especially love your loving Valentine gift:
You paid for my perky boobs to have an extra groovy lift.
And I love the way you treated me to have my lips full done too:
Oh my sweet sugar daddy, there is no limit and no end
to what for me you do.
And when I went to the beauty salon for lots of daring body piercing
and sexy tattooing:
You told me not to worry about what all the other girls were doing.
Telling me to just have done what I wanted to have well done:
Like your tender love for me there is no limit to me having
young girly fun.
And I love all your other loving Valentines which made my heart sing:
A silky selection of red heart-shaped see-through thong things
With a swinging glowing pearl string.
It gave me such a daring thrill sliding into such flimsy frilly delights:
Which I love wearing all sultry days and romantic starry nights.
For I know I'm only eighteen young summers and you're sixty-three;
Yet there is something about an older autumn season lover
That brings me such sweet heart-pounding ecstasy!

And when you told me that I was your loving and living Valentine;
I knew that though you're rather too slow at times,
You know how to love me in a tantalising way that's totally divine!
I know you think I'm rather bold and naughty
When I wear my bare bum teaser hipster navel flaunting skirts;
Slung low down at my hip to show my dimple belly button line to flirt
And high of hem showing just a glimpse of my heart-shaped
thong string:
But you know that I will ever be your special teenage Valentine girl;
And I love the much older man that's you, for you ever have my heart
beating fast as each new pleasure you unfurl!'

Jackie J Docherty

A Special Valentine

You are my light,
you are my love,
you're in every blessing,
received from above.
You are my sunrise,
my stars in the night,
the one in this world,
who makes my life bright . . .
You are my smile,
my tears and my laughter,
you are my today,
and all hereafter . . .
So on this day,
saved for love that's true,
I want you to know,
just how much I love you!

Kitty Morgan

A VALENTINE TO REMEMBER

I sit alone on this seat
As romantic couples pass me by
Arm in arm, full of love
I can see they are wondering, why?

It's Valentine's Day
She shouldn't be sitting there alone
Not in lover's corner
At St Valentine's stone

But it's here where me first met
Exactly 10 years ago
We held each other on this stone
And vowed never to let go

You were my one and only true love
And nothing could touch us
In our two short years together
We lived life with a buzz

As you were taken from my life
I never let you see me cry
I was grateful for the time we had together
Memories I could treasure as I watched you die

So please don't pity me
As you pass by my way
I feel his love all around me
This and every Valentine's Day.

Rachael Cowham

TRUE ANGEL

Why do we care when we hurt so much?
We need to feel love,
And a tender touch,
The sadness and sorrow that breaks up our heart,
The torture and pain,
That rips us apart,
We muddle through life, don't know what's to come,
Crying out loud,
Are they worth it? Not one!
To be one so sad; so depressed in this land,
I need so much love,
To take life by the hand,
Then he appears; with his heavenly glow,
His wings soft and white,
Like the cold winter's snow!
Towering above me he sits by my side,
Taking my hand,
We fly into the night,
To a land full of peace; there's no trouble anymore,
I can see a long path,
That will lead to a door.
Once he opens this door and sets my hearts free,
No longer will sadness,
Overcome me!
So with Heaven above, and hell down below,
I am now a true angel,
With wings white as snow . . .

Janet Brook

I HAVE A LOVER...

I have a lover
Who had slipped into my life so silently . . .

I think of him, feel him touch me,
And when I close my eyes
My body trembles at the memory of him,
Aching that secret ache in places he has touched.

I so long to hold him,
To taste his lips
(Oh those precious lips, such a focus of my desire!)
To feel his body close to mine,
Moulding each to the other,
Fulfilling all previous torments,
Yet, creating only more.

Oh I have a lover,
And when he touches me,
I fear the light he ignites in me,
Making me weak, so weak,
That he holds me, suspended, floating,
In that twilight world, so simply ours.

I drown in him, savouring his touch,
The passion he gives creating the peace I crave,
Teasing my spirit and bringing me into him,
I lose myself in these moments of sheer pleasure.

Oh I have a lover . . .

Wendy Gray

WHEN WE SLEEP

When we sleep I miss you most,
But we are not apart,
My dreams are a new world,
Filled with you,
I'm drawn to your eyes,
As deep as the oceans blue,
My feet wander down to your shore,
I dive in,
To swim in the sea that is your love,
Surrounded by everything you are,
The security of your warm embrace,
Fingertips of silk,
Make me shiver,
Your breath on my neck,
Carries me up high,
To float on clouds,
I'm looking down,
I'm falling into you.

Richard Ward

LOVE'S DAY
(Dedicated to sweet Wilma Grundy)

Momentous days are few and far between -
But this stands out a mile;
St Valentine - who was he? - never knew
What fervour stemmed from him.

But wait - St Valentine has no hold over me!
I make my own decisions,
The best of which was when I chose to love
Sweet Wilma Grundy!

But did I choose - or was the feeling sent
From higher planes?
The answer is that I may never know
From where the blessing came.

Enough of romance - now let me try to be
A realist - for once!
The chances of reciprocal response
Are slim, to say the least.

But 'faint heart never won fair maid', it's said,
So let me take this chance,
And broadcast my fine ardour to the world -
Which doesn't give a damn!

Sandy Splitt

OFF BY HEART

Some people learn

poems
speeches
Shakespeare

'off by heart'
(It can be romantic!)

unlike you -

you've learnt my pants.

Nicola C Grant

MY FUNNY VALENTINE

I wanna write
A poem,
I really, really
Do
But somehow feelings
Are all mixed up
And it's *all*
Because of you.
You madden me -
You gladden me -
At times
My heart can sing
If only dearest sweetheart
Some chocolate
You would *bring!*

Lyn Sandford

Do You Feel This Way?

Now we're together I need search no more
I'm with you and it was certainly worth waiting for
I can't believe that I've found a love so true
My life is worth nothing if I can't be with you
Tell me, do you feel this way?

True love and companionship is what we've got
The way I feel for you is more than a lot
A future together for us is what I see
And faithful to each other is what we will be
Tell me, do you feel this way?

So darling, take care of me your whole life through
Say you'll always love me like I will you
I want to face the challenge with you whatever life may hold
Spend each passing day with you whilst together we grow old
You know, I'll always feel this way.

Victoria F J Welton

WIFE 'MY VALENTINE'

No longer do I say those silly phrases
Roses are red violets are blue,
The only words she wants to hear
Darling, I love you.

She may not be a blushing rose
She's now three score and four,
Her eyes still twinkle, now, as then,
For reasons different, I love her more.

My wife has always been my Valentine
And I, her Romeo,
Through the years, kept lit the fire,
That roused in me my first desires.

Fading beauty in her autumn years
Still she turns to gold,
Magic still there, as when I first saw
In my youth before I became old.

No longer do I say those silly phrases
Roses are red violets are blue,
If I had to choose the same again
No other would I pick, but you.

P A McDonnell

I WISH I WERE

I wish I were like Superman,
As I could fly to you,
Or maybe, on a motorbike,
As that, would do me too.

I wish I were, a garden worm,
A-tunnelling, in the ground,
I would tunnel, and I'd keep on going,
Until, yes you I found.

I wish I were, a little cloud,
A-floating, in the sky,
I'd float to you, and you know what,
I would not, pass you by.

I'd like to be, a big fat pigeon,
In full flight, through the air,
A straight flight, all the way to you,
Without a stop or care.

I wish I were electricity,
Running through mains cable,
I'd run to your house, all the way,
And shock you, if I were able.

But I'd rather be a stray tomcat,
Prowling round the streets,
I'd prowl around until again,
Yes, somehow, you, I'd meet.

But what better, if I were me right now,
Sitting, next to you
On my face, would be the biggest smile,
For this, I would tell you true.

I love you truly, greatly and sweet,
My love, is one vast well,
I guess it's true, you know the saying,
Valentine, my heart for you, has fell.

C R Slater

GIFTS

Money provides security
and reduces desperation
tobacco steadies tattered nerves
and ensures good respiration
alcohol warms chilly limbs
and lubricates our relations
music compels hips to swing
and brings on good vibrations
but love; love's a symphony for the soul
sparkles the eyes, completes the whole
love is a lens through which we see
love, my dear, is your gift to me

Me? I cause insecurity
and amplify desperation
I shred once infallible nerves
and falter your respiration
I steal duvets from chilly limbs
and cause frosty relations
I compel strong stomachs to turn
and bring on horrid sensations
but love, love you cannot control
it creeps up and consumes you whole
love is the gift I offer you
I'll drive you mad; what can you do?

Paul S Dawson

SCHOLAR TO HER BEAUTY

She lives in a hue of calm
She sings of hope and reason
Her dance a captive grace
Her eyes magic and deep.

So young is she
This summer flower
Elegant and fine
Like a petal upon a breeze.
So whole and true
In her addictive splendour,
I thrive to taste the essence of she.

Just her name starts wheels turning
Pulling back shades upon reality
If I'm a scholar to her beauty
Then let her name set knowledge free.

Shapes change
Bring reflections
All things that I live to be,
All my dreams
Fears and longings,
I know to her
I can truly speak.

Paul Fulton

ABBA-ESQUE AND THE CAPTAIN OF MY HEART
(To Andrew)

Trawling through the
super slinky-lipped print of
the want ads I come across
a destination in lonely hearts
plump wish words juicy with
lists of requirements divulge
the Birmingham bagged flares of
Bay City Roller man or similar

northern soul eyes protrude
a little larger into my gyrating heart
on receipt of unscrubbed photo from
a dog-eared lens and the capture of
a pair of West Coast jeans from
their groove loving zipped blue centre and the
icicle pierce of a riff from a Quo
tune reminds me of

your unaftershaved face like on
a hundred seventies album covers
dragging me over T-bone dinner miles
from home and
taking my coat as a forethought
in a cosy pub corner far from the
maddeningly unbelievable political perfection
of late twentieth century inoffense what with
you paying and me getting
flowers on top I wonder
where you were when Abba sang Waterloo.

Julie Ashpool

ONLY LOVE

Though storms may rage
Water may fall
I shall kiss thy memories
Unforgotten by time and age.

James Patrick Milton

VALENTINE

One peered across a satin rose, its stature revolved around the globe of alighting sapphire tips of ice-cooled champagne bubbling inside a crystal crown, gems were found, perceptive senses, tantalised requited, for it was a fear, ironic discomfort, luring promises with delicate touches, the air silk colliding and reminding of breezes, sunlit forest, revamped choices in a moment of elegance and harmony's plea to be with the nature that is thee.

Jamie McBeath

TONIGHT

Tossing your love,
on the tide of loneliness,
like a moon,
on the stream at night.
The talisman of your touch
piercing deep down
my drowned heart,
lifting my soul
in the magical incantation
of your voice,
alluring as a nightingale,
singing sweetly
in the wake of love.

Senator Ihenyen

LOVE IN CONCERT

In the evening then
her slender figure in that long black gown,
her fair plait glimmering,
her trumpet pressed against
her breast,
her belly breathing and
her baby blues
promising.

Timothy McNeal

. . . AND TODAY, ON LOVER'S DAY . . .

(For my wife Jan
The only Valentine I'll ever need)

. . . I long for your arms holding me again,
I long to feel your soft breath upon my chest
and my heartbeat to echo within your twinkling eyes;

I long to feel your fingers stroking my hair
and your sweet lips pursed and pressed upon mine;
I long to feel the vibration of your heaving breast
against my body, creating those bodily endorphins
we know will result in love, oh, such love

. . . and today, on lover's day,
I shall love you in every way
as I always have done
and will, till, the dying of the sun . . .

tcmoon

THE TWO FLAMINGOS

My adoration of you dear wife and friend
spans over 50 years to date, during which
time our mutual feeling never dwindled,
instead grew and grew to new heights of love,
decidedly of different kind, each time.

My Valentine would then be:
no storms and turmoils can ever destroy
our well earned empathy and friendship as
our companionship well withstood the
proof of time - QED.

P P Christodoulides

BED OF ROSES

I want you
to lay me down
on a bed of roses.

I want you
to hold me tight
on a bed of roses.

I want you
to caress my body
on a bed of roses.

I want you
to make love to me
on a bed of roses.

Catrina Lawrence

PARIS VALENTINE

The gentleman smiled and said, 'Hello'
The lady gave a teasing laugh,
And waved to the man she did not know.
He wished he could be more refined,
She wished she could be more on time
For her appointment.
This was the first time that they met,
She made an impression on him that he would not forget.
How warm the sunshine made him feel
And yet, how good it was to be in Paris.
Yes, she also wanted to reveal
To all the passers by, how much she loved Paris.

The next time that they met,
The gentleman introduced himself,
As a musician playing for the Orchestra de France.
She was walking by the River Seine,
And did not want to miss the chance,
Of getting to know him.
She was on teaching vacation it seemed
And he was working in Paris.
They walked and talked of the plans they dreamed,
Until the hours had gone by -
And he had to depart.

'Be my Valentine' was all he could say,
When he met her the very next day.
She smiled in a wistful way,
And accepted his proposal.
This is the romantic City
Where doves fly high in the sky,
Girls are so pretty, and poets write prose.

And music, like the River Seine flows.
Romance flourishes and grows.
In this perfect setting
Was where she became his Valentine Rose.

Hilarie Grinnell

EVERY DAY IS SPECIAL

Every day is special with you dear in my heart
You know how much I love you I have loved you from the start.

Every day is special you bring me happiness and joy
You gave me beautiful children two girls and a little boy.

Every day is special I feel twelve feet tall
You make me oh so happy dear every day it is a ball.

Every day is special you make me feel so grand
When you sing to me your love songs
While we're walking hand in hand.

Every day is special it has been since we met
My love for you will never die on that my dear you bet.

Every day is special every second we spend together
As I love you oh so much my love will last forever.

Kram

MADRIGAL

A thousand dreams ago,
I heard a minstrel play
His airs of love.
With lute gently plucked,
He sang in sweetest notes
Of love, of joy, of hope.

A thousand dreams ago,
My hand in thine I placed,
My heart to thee I gave,
Taking his theme of love
Into a sunlit glade.
He bowed as we passed by,
Gave us that lovely day.

A thousand dreams ago,
I heard a minstrel play.

Audrey J Roberts

NEPTUNE DREAMS

Leaning back on the warm sand
he closes his eyes.

The swell's alluring and gentle still,
he slips beneath the surface and sweeps
outward carried now by the under rush
of the wave, racing past trails of seaweed
embedded shells and rounded pebbles.
His powerful stroke drives him on, the seabed
is moving swiftly past him, a wave goes over
he feels the pressure rise and fall, he lifts
into the cleft, all quiet now, enclosed
by smooth mounds in front and behind.

High, he hugs the wave and is borne over
its soft curve, the next ahead a rising hill
with a small break on the crest. Up and up
then falling slowly to the ocean's rhythm
he rests in the troughs, then dives deep down,
moving through the warm currents, stretched,
extended as a swordfish, then half out of the water
he's flying over the top arms spread like a gannet
taking to the air. Relaxing he feels the gentle
touch of water on his skin, caring, caressing
slipping through the hairs of his chest.

He turns, is lifted high from behind,
the wave breaks tossing him lightly
forward, bubbles lick him as he is
lowered again. He breathes faster,
then a big one comes, rising, breaking
it lifts and rolls him over and over,
round and round he goes, till he greets
the air again and gasps as he is set back
in the soft valley, though now the sand
and shingle are rushing past below, chest
and legs tingling with their tremors;

another and he is moving quietly,
slowly toward the shore where
he is laid upon the beach.

He stirred, his love still there,
he, his head upon her lap, she,
leaning forward, her fingers
idly rippling through
the hair on his chest.

Gordon Stewart

YOU

You are my beginning
You are my ending
You are my completeness
My everything

You are the morning
You are the evening
You are in the words
Of the songs that I sing

You are my breath
You are my heartbeat
You are in every single
Movement I make

You are in my mind
You are in my spirit
You are with me always
Asleep and awake

You are the reason
You are the season
You are the summer, autumn
Winter and spring

You are my purpose
You are my meaning
You are my completeness
My everything.

Barbara Manning

THE GLASS ROSE
(Dedicated to Jenni Hussain)

Just a small glass rose
Upon a shelf -
It seemed to beckon me.

I gazed at it
All shining bright
And somehow thought of thee!

On upright stem -
Bloom held aloft -
It sparkled in the light!

Slight tint of pink
So delicate -
'Twas such a lovely sight!

I chose that rose
Of molten glass
And held it gently in my hand.

I took it home
And packed it up
To send to your fair hand.

Each time you see
This pretty rose
As it is standing there -

I hope you'll know
I think of you -
And know I truly care!

Cor-E Barras

GROWING OLD TOGETHER

Beloved,
Sleeping quietly beside me,
Heart synchronised to mine,
Beating . . .
Beating . . .
Breathing . . .
Breathing . . .
Together.
There are moments,
Shimmering pools of consciousness,
When I reflect on life's gifts,
For what surety can there be,
That fate will grace us
With another day?
Hearts beating . . .
Beating . . .
Breathing . . .
Breathing . . .
Growing old together.

Cyndie Goins Hoelscher

LOVE IS LIGHT

If the sun fades and goes, never to return
The world will be in darkness.
No more colours to see, black against dark.
If you are by my side the radiance from your heart
Will lighten the world and the colours will return.

Duncan MacFarlane

CRYPTIC WORDS FOR YOUR SWEETHEART

LOVE
LOV   A sweetheart
LO
L

AIRY
AIR   Is fanciful
AI
A

ALSO
ALS   And
AL
A

VIEW
VIE   Looks
VI
V

ISLE
ISL   Towards the isle
IS
I

ABLE
ABL   They are able
AB
A

AEON
AEO   To have an immense time
AE
A

ATOM
 ATO   With energy.
  AT
   A

ATOM
 ATO   Lots of energy
  AT
   A

AEON
 AEO   For an impassioned immense time
  AE
   A

ARCH
 ARC   They have a wonderful arch smile
  AR
   A

Maria Ann Cahill

VALENTINES

I look at the cards and flowers
In the shops
And feel lonely.
Even though logic tells me
It's commercial hype.
I have no one to send anything to . . .
No expectations of receiving . . .
There is someone I love,
But my true feelings
Must remain trapped
Like a butterfly beating its wings
In a chloroform jar
To speak of my love,
May chase my friend away.
So actions must speak louder
And I hope realisation
Comes to settle one day.
And I opened the cruel jar
And the butterfly
She flew away
To nestle in my heart
I feel her often
Tiny beating wings
When my loved one's close.

Liz Osmond

THE POTTED GIFT

It arrived on Valentine's Day
Blooming red with green petals
Shaped like pineapple leaves.
The deep colour matching my Shalwar Kameez.
It filled my room with bright rays of light.
A centrepiece, in its own pale ceramic pot.
Each time I passed it I touched it
Interchanging passion, as I watched tiny droplets
Drip down like a waterfall
Until they reached the soil below.
It gave me months of pleasure,
And years if I'd let it.
But I started to neglect it.
And the tips of its leaves began to turn in
And fade. I stopped watering or feeding it.
I watched it slowly die.
I should have thrown it away, but I couldn't.
Its stiff leaves now limp, turned towards the ground,
Its Valentine colour now gone.
I placed it on the floor in the corner of the room
Hidden, only I knew it was there.
The roots still immersed in the soil that was now its grave
I despised it, but I couldn't take away its place in my room.
All I could do now was look at it and remember it was once a deep red.

Ravina Ryder

THE SPIDER AND THE FLY

You're leaving this time for a long time
How will I survive without you?
I'll miss your laughing twinkling eyes
And the way you loved me too.

I'll wait for you forever my love
Even though our love must die
For I'm surely stuck to your web
You're the spider and I'm the fly.

No matter where you are in the world
My memory of you will be strong
I'll still love you even after death
Maybe then our love won't be wrong!

My heart and soul is forever yours
I'll never find love like yours again
My heart will always belong to you
You're the sweetest of all men.

Each time we go to the airport
I want to stay with you until you go
To watch at the window and wave
But I find it hard to let love show.

Each time we have to say goodbye
There's so much I want to say
But if I try to say too much
Then I'd be begging you to stay!

Your culture forbids us to marry
But we'll meet again when we die
For I'm surely stuck to your web
You're the spider and I'm the fly!

Rose Murdoch

TWIN FLAME

A spark flickers sporadically,
Adrift in a vast ocean,
Lost,
Alone,
Searching unfulfilled,

Fate intervenes,
Two sparks collide,
Ignite,
Steadily growing,
In unison blending,

Swaying,
Intertwining,
Spiralling upward,
United,
Into one flame,

A burning fire of emotion,
Soaring to new heights,
Joined,
In the ecstasy of the moment,
Void of ego,

At one,
In desire,
Bound,
By an unseen force,
Twin flames,

Cast adrift, aeons ago,
At the beginning of time,
And destined to reunite once more,
In the future,
To be connected for eternity.

Ann G Wallace

MY SWEET VALENTINE

Sweet you are,
My lovely valentine,
I think of your love,
All of the time.

Everything I do,
Is inspired by you,
My first love and last,
From my dark distant past.

One day we will marry,
And our souls will entwine,
Our bodies together,
Will make us feel fine.

All the love in my heart,
I will give to you,
We will never be apart,
This is my promise to you.

Love is a great gift,
The greatest of all,
And your love to me,
Makes me stand tall.

My head is up high,
Nose in the air,
Knowing you love me,
And really care.

Yes, you are sweet,
My valentine,
I have thoughts of your love,
All of the time.

I treasure every moment,
We spend alone,
Talking and loving you,
I really have grown.

Please my sweet love,
Oh never leave,
I couldn't stand the pain,
When I start to grieve.

There's not a lot more,
I really could say,
Except that my darling,
Love's here to stay.

S Longford

THROUGH THIS WINDOW

In this past year, I've gazed across my wine,
Into your loving eyes and o'er your shoulder,
Where, through this window, I have seen the seasons change
And reminisced of sights and sounds we've seen.

The snow was heavy on the cedar's boughs,
When first I gazed through frosted windowpanes,
And we were leaving for the Christmas Ice Rink
To soak up festive season's joyous atmosphere.

Spring buds and flowers were blooming at the window
And we held hands on lakeside walks,
The hope of spring in both our hearts,
As winter's grey turned brighter in the sun.

The dazzling sun glanced off the window's glass,
When we called in from summer trips,
With sea breezed hair and sun-kissed faces,
Relaxing here in evening's quiet reverie,

Autumn's colours appeared outside this window,
And thicker sweaters warmed us in the wind,
Country walks were cooler but as special
And early, cosy, firelight welcomed us again,

Now snow is on the cedar's boughs once more
And Christmas lights are twinkling in the night,
This wondrous year, as I gaze through this window,
Will stay within my heart for evermore.

The loving, precious timeless thoughts and feelings,
That we have shared in many different ways,
The places, through each season, ever memorable,
Held in our hearts, our souls and dreams, our minds.

So I have watched, full circle, through this window,
All the seasons, we have seen and touched,
And walked and laughed and loved with you,
For these and all of those, I thank you darling one.

Glyn Davies

DEAR HEART

It seemed I walked in darkness, unloved, lost,
Until I met you dearest heart, my love,
A past love washed upon a distant coast,
Had left me broken-hearted, left to rove.
How could I have not seen the dewdrops bright,
The distant rainbow's colours, painted skies,
Not heard the thrushes song, the swans in flight,
Not seen your love for me in sparkling eyes,
You hold my hand so gently dearest heart,
And speak so softly, thoughts unspoken heard,
Awoke my love, unlocked my aching heart,
Removed the darkened veil, for love I yearned.
I sleep, my hair you caress, dreams I dream,
Our souls are one dear heart, always to dream.

David M Walford

INSIDE OUT PROPOSAL

Notice me please! I feel that you must
know how I expose myself
to write this Valentine - spotlight lit.

Look at the clothes that give you a key
showing you all there is to know about me.

Feel the cloth and see the cut of it,
made to measure, not off the shelf;
love can never be blown away like dust.

Take me as seen, let there be no confusions
as nothing about me is done for effect.
My words of love are truly meant.

The truth of their purpose will never falter;
the thrust of our passion will lead to the altar.

I love and adore you! don't rent
my intentions to gain your respect
to live our lives without illusions.

One look at you makes my eyes shine
as you shall be forever my Valentine.

Michael Fenton

CROWN ME MRS

Crown me Mrs.
For years I have played the role
And it's only fair
That you officially give me my title
'Cause neither one of us seem to be going anywhere
Too much at stake
Too much invested
Time
Emotions
Finances
Love
I want more!
We played house long enough
I say we up the ante
And make it official
Get some paperwork on this thing
It's mutually beneficial
Been together for too long
Through many ups and downs
Was in constant support of you
When no one else was around
Every ear hears but not every ear listens
You'd better wake up
I'm ready to be crowned Mrs.
Will not continue to be common law
Ain't no benefits in that!
Shacking up with no rights upon you that's not where it's at
Legalise my position
Give me what's rightfully due to me
The crown of love

Permanence
And security
Or you'll soon find yourself missing
My lovin'
My voice
My touches
My kisses
The consequences of not being crowned Mrs.
I've given you an offspring with your last name
But my last name still remains the same
See you want your cake and you want to eat it too
Have me on lock-down
While you're doing you
You can't live like you're committed and live like you're single too
I'm the best you're gonna get
The chicken heads and gold-diggers haven't proven that to you yet?
This is my promise, so pay attention and listen
I'm out of here with the quickness.
Unless you decide to crown me Mrs.

Tonya Barber

SOLDIER'S VALENTINE 1949

Welbeck, so called Abbey
with its underground passages
built by out of work miners
for philanthropic nobleman.

Later, home to an idea -
to rehabilitate soldiers
for a peacetime role
and return to normality.

Famed underground ballroom
and drawing rooms of aristocracy
turned into studios, lecture venue
and craft workshops.

Here they would relearn
professional working, new thinking,
craft and practical skills,
preparing their return.

Return to community,
to home life, family and friends,
to Civvy Street, office, factory, college
and that girl.

Deep in those creepy studios below,
in dark of night, a budding artist
pens a loving note
and paints a special Valentine.

Startling sounds! The Abbey wraith
floats past nervous sentries
and scatters tipsy soldiery
outside the NAAFI.

Other curious soldiers
disturb the artist's concentration.
Dust sheet covers love's blandishments
until intruders depart.

Into a stiffened envelope
The romantic work of art is pressed,
marked boldly 'Do not fold!'
Will it survive the postman's malice?

By return comes her reply:
Twin hearts entwined on stationer's card.
Stereotyped, maybe,
but sentiment just as true.

Jo Allen

MARIA

Follow that sunbeam and that sunflower,
A smile like a huge dam and river;
and a big, blue sky.
She tells the whole world of her troubled woes,
Of her romances and of all of her fallen dreams.
Maria, she is gold to be taken away;
on a ride to Cyprus Island.
Her kindness is so solid, like Earth
and she has the strength of beauty.
But beware of Maria, she can trap you like a bear.
You try to flatter her with flowers,
just beware she is a woman.
Maria, my friendly female,
who's number one in all men's hearts,
She loves all animals too.

Richard Chapman

THE FIRST LOVE

His hair was bright red, his eyes were so blue,
One look and my heart gave a leap, it's true.
We met, we touched, we loved.
How could this be?
I don't like red hair but my heart says yes for me.
It wasn't meant to last,
While it did, I was enchanted.
Then I met a lad with dark hair
And so red and I parted.
Now often, as I'm old
I think of that first lover.
We used to wander far
And loved in fields of clover.
Does he ever think of me -
What life we could have led?
As I often sit and wonder
If only! How often this is said.

Marj Busby

MY VALENTINE

When love commands understanding,
The door to the heart stands open wide,
When romance comes a-roving,
In sweet paradise, oh sweet paradise.

Nothing really matters, Oh my Valentine,
But to have loved is the greatest feeling,
When shared with the one you love,
Like all the sparkling stars up in Heaven.

Love always feels very nice,
To my sweet Valentine,
Your natural beauty is so divine,
So carefree, so naturally and mine.

In nature's beautiful garden,
Across warm sunny bowers,
Where Utopia is dreamy beneath sunny showers,
Love freely blossoms with the feelings of eureka.

Inside one's breast, the heart flutters in time,
With attainments, beauties and words that rhyme,
Where the English poet kisses his sweetheart
Upon the green lawns of paradise.

Knowing only the words of sweet love,
And a sweet picture inside a locked cameo,
To keep a happy secret, between two,
Is but a dream, manufactured up in Heaven.

Where white fluffy clouds pass on by,
Where a beautiful rainbow arc is seen.
So bright and magical, with natural colours,
Painted and designed especially for lovers.

Wherever they may go, like sweet, happy children,
Playing in the park, with mirth and gaiety.
So wondrous, so delightful with purity in mind,
As they walk hand in hand across nature's natural landscape.

Is it not a wonder, why lovers unite,
With happy fond memories,
Of yesteryears walk,
Where beautiful birds fly with outstretched wings.

This is the fairy kingdom of the Earth,
Where all magic is bestowed,
Unspoiled with perfection and celestial,
Where Angels of Eden walk singing spiritually.

James Stephen Cameron

SHADES OF TENDERNESS

A golden - brown time of year,
She's dancing to the rhythm of the blues.
Tinges of winter grey clouds fill her eyes as
Softly rolling September fades away
Into lapis lazuli skies.

Pink lips and ruby kisses swirl around in his head
White noise and coloured lights reverberate
Around the room.
Flowing, the movement of her scarlet dress
Will fill his dreams tonight.

His head softly resting on
Her snow-white breast.

Vicky Stevens

ON MY KNEE

I'll wait a while here on my knee as the sun yawns and nestles down behind me. I'll listen for the song of the barn owl's prayer and the rustle of the badger's nose as night-time silences the friendly chatter of the birds.

I'll wait a while here on my knee as the summer breeze invites her friend, the autumnal wind, to caress my face and burn my ears. I'll watch the leaves turn yellow and gold, as winter lays her blanket through the audience of trees that never complain of the cold and rain.

I'll wait a while here on my knee as the children return in springtime, a good rabbit taller, passing a knowing look to the timeless branches of the old cedar tree. Their faces broader, with a wiser look that only appears when one knows one can now tie one's own shoe laces.

I'll wait a while here on my knees as a full year peaks over the roof of the woods, smiling kindly as if to say, 'Are you still here? She must be very special.' I reply silently with a nod and half a smile.

I'll wait a while here on my knee for the words that I now live for, when you come to kneel down next to me, smile and whisper, 'Yes, I will.'

Colin D Chapman

LOVE

You fill my heart in such a way
I really can't explain
On impact it's confusing
But when I contemplate it's plain

It's mental and it's physical
A gift from up above
And if I had to put it in a word
I'd have to say it's love!

Georgina Paraskeva

NOT WITHOUT YOU
(Dedicated to Lizzie, my lovely wife)

I would never have made it this far
Without you.
You are my lady
And the hidden star
Behind most things I do.

You arrived at a point in time
When I wasn't strong.
I stood at a cross-roads,
Uncertain about direction.
Then you showed me the light;
A guiding beacon,
And with the power of your love
I knew I could try again.

Since then I've never looked back,
You are always around to guide me
Along the track.
So it really is true,
That I would never have made it this far
Without you - my lady star.

Ron Whatley

SEA SONG

'There's more than one fish in the sea, so they say
There's more than one fish in the sea.
But from all that I've learned, where love is concerned,
There will only be one for me.
So fishermen fish, wherever you wish,
For I've already cast my line.
And here I shall wait, 'til she swims for my bait
And becomes my Valentine.

Alan Millard

MY FUNNY VALENTINE

Agonising over flowers and cards brought no results,
It wasn't that I didn't care: I thought of it too much.

Jewelry and personal treasures came next, compounding doubts:
I'd buy a ring you'd never wear or choose dark chocolates.

So here I am: no gift or card . . .
Too late to organise that special meal by candlelight -
Sweetheart, the thought is there, but love is all I've brought.

Patrick B Osada

FATAL LOVE

I love you
You know I do
I tell you every day
Don't I?

Well I do
Everyday a bit more
Like leprosy

But, and this is a totally separate issue
If you must snore again tonight
every night
Then my love
I simply must
Kill you.

Nicolette Turner

VALENTINE

In my deserted life
You are the only oasis
Your love is like spring clouds
Shielding me from scorching sun
When my life was empty
You filled it with your love
When I was burning with sorrows
You showered your gentle love
You are a spring's touch
That melts the wintry frost
Believe me
I love you so much!
Deep inside my heart
I know that even though we are apart
But the barriers standing between us
Will not weaken our love
My love will hold you, protect you, comfort you
In your blues
You can feel me near you all the time
'Cause I am your heartbeat
So this I let you know
That I shall keep my love safe
From the eyes of the harsh world
And when this life is over
We'll be together forever
Like two eternal lovers . . .

Qurat-ul-Ain Rizvi

A SATURDAY AFTERNOON
(For J)

I know what bliss is,
I must conclude,
'Tis your sweet kisses,
With Chinese food.

Mark Bailey

EQUATION

I never though that I could be worthy of a love so right and good
when I first looked deep into your eyes
Time stood still
When you first kissed my mouth
My heart stood still
You are my life for now and always
For my love is as measurable as infinity multipled
by the square root of eternity
I love you

Mairi Tognin

LOVE!

Love is to show a tear; love is to
    hold you near.

Love is to feel the pain; love is
    to feel the same.

Love is to have and hold; love is
    given and not sold.

Love is to open your mind; love is
    to not be blind.

Love is to have and cherish; love is
    to never perish.

Jayson J Moran

VALENTINE

You can never know who I am
Only that I love you
And our hearts will never dance as one
The briefest courtesy
Is all that will ever pass between us
The light that fills me
When I make you smile
Can only last a moment
Not the years that I long for

James Olley

REBUTTAL

Your eyes
look at me and
the world stops, deep golden
promises, syrup flies sip
and die.

Your lips,
dark foxglove-pink,
smile and your teeth show white
as icebergs sparked by sun, breathing
a lie.

Your cheeks
clear glowing pearl
soft-blushed with rose, predict
a dawn of loveliness. Beware
such skies.

Dark brows
and honey hair
beguile my heart with warmth,
stripping me bare and tangling me
ensnared.

Your voice
the wash of surf
along the sand, soothing
embrace, hiding the tidal wave's
dread surge.

And you,
beauty enfleshed,
freedom of songbirds' wings,
glide on the air and singing ride
the wind.

Pat Earnshaw

THERE YOU ARE

Spider-web
Drawer-deep
Quiet love
Threads
A shirt
Laundered

I hear your footsteps
On the pavement of my mind
And, turning,
Hear your laughter in the hills,
Your sorrows
In the buzzard's cry.

Alan Chesterfield

DEDICATED TO DAVID

Greying now,
Slowly maturing,
Distinguished -
I gaze on you,
My dear 'old thing'.

Remembering
The very start -
A glance,
That smile;
You stole my heart.

Unexpectedly
Into my life
You came,
Bringing sunshine,
Making me a wife.

Seeing you -
Still a thrill
Every day
As back then;
For I love you still.

Geri Laker

IF

(A Valentine to my husband)

If I was a bird,
I'd fly to thee
Singing of my love;
Emptying my heart
Of its longing for thee.

If I was a mist,
I'd softly creep
To enfold thee
And hold thee
In soft embrace.

But
I am your joy,
My thoughts go winging
Like a bird;
My dreams enfold thee
Like a mist.
And I do love thee
For ever.

Audrey J Roberts

FOR BRIGHT EYES

There was true belief when
Departure took place one noon
Those adamant eyes, so bright
To light every gene in spirit;
Revealed how the roots of
Love did exist in you.
It is those eyes this
Pen did worship all these
Days, as ancient rishis in
Deep divine prayers of Omkara.
The manthra that unabandoning eyes
Did transmit with those rays,
Emitted in quanta discrete, did
Pierce and prompt those moments in
This idle soul that never
Ventured to depict this way.

Alby Raymond Parackal

WHISPERS IN THE DARK

I kissed you today
In the cool of the morning
When lips hardly part
Because love had its say
In the night, in the dark
Of a whispered reunion
To the child in our heart
That continues to play.

In the night you are mine
And by dawn I am yours
Yet the day of the breath of your life
Tears a carousel line
Of tangles and tears,
Worry, trouble and strife.
If the joy of this course
Is being your wife
Where's the man in the Valentine?

Clare Saffell

ANY HUMAN WOULD

The beauty she looks you straight in the eye
Are you so blind, cannot see
That for you she would die
I know that she has done wrong
I know that she has sinned
But any human would

But remember the smiles, the laughs and the rest
Forget all the tears and heartache and pain
The beauty she stares you straight in the eye
Please just forgive her
Any human would.

Cate Harris

VALENTINE BUTTERFLIES

As that day
of secret love
draws near
the excitement of
anticipation hits
my inner stomachs
shaking walls,
where crashing

disturbed mad
butterflies
dog fight
in the light
of a fluttering
burning flame.

I stand unsettled,
restricted by
insecure doubt, a
passionate believer
of nervousness, but

then that greeting
card reassures, kiss
festooned with
future aspirations,
as the fluttering glides
to gently calm, for
they now hover, land
and slowly settle,
wings folded,
touching, erect,
before the angel lift
to homewards,
heart-bound fly.

Ian Bowen

I HAVE A SECRET

I have a secret in my heart
Look hard and try to puzzle
Out my message, if you're really smart
Verse is all I need to hide,
Each word and take you for a ride.
You may not figure it out in rhyme
Or else, in time you may just spring
Upon my hidden Valentine.

I'll see you in the springtime
In the blossoming of love
I'll hear you in the phrases
Of our feathered friends above;
I'll share the warmth of summer
In the brightness of your eyes
I'll chase you in the falling leaves
Beneath the autumn skies,
I'll shelter you from frosting
Through nights in wintertime
Till spring returns I'll keep you
If you'll be my Valentine.

Evelyn Leite

UNDIMINISHED

You call me
       draw me to your desire

You caress me
       with your scent-oiled voice

You bathe my body firmly
       handle me with care

You unmake me
       make me up to our old recipe

You know me again
       in every way and nook

Refuelled -
       re-fired -
I acquiesce in love.

Sue Britchford

MY LIFE'S LOVE

I sent you a card
you stood it on the TV
you didn't even open it

I bought you a card
all I wrote on it:
I love you

I told it all on a card
after twenty-three years
some happy, some hard

I wished on a card
but you weren't listening
and you left the next year . . .

My love for life . . .

Renate Fekète

DECEPTION

For months
I've been telling myself
that six months
isn't a long time.
But now,
as the dates ripen,
I'm counting the days.

John Kay

LOVE AT FIRST SIGHT
(Dedicated to John Stephen Dimond)

It was love at first sight
The day that we met
You were gentle and shy
I'll never forget
We courted a while
Our love surely grew
It was sure meant to be
I was destined for you
But complications happened
And we grew apart
Yet feelings for you
Still lay deep in my heart
Many years passed
You remained in my mind
I still remembered you
Thoughtful and kind
You've stayed in my heart
I'll never forget
The day I first met you
Right from the start
Fate brought us back
We're together to stay
Many years later
I heard people say
It was meant to be
For that couple there
They were meant to be
They're the perfect pair.

Nicola Joy Moore

Naval Cadet's Sweetheart

The very young guardiamarina has not fallen in love
with Janes, Nicoles or Sabrinas.
He has fallen in love with Marinas!
The naval cadet said to his old friend,
'Marinas are unusual girls,
Their appearance and mind are best,
Among the girls of the west!'
And the golden ring with aquamarine,
Is shining on the finger of guardiamarina,
It was the nice gift of Marina!
The guardiamarina took the field to Chinese coasts,
Where power was had in hand of mandarins,
And about three years he could not forget Marina!

Petr Nicolayevich Maltsev

MY BEAUTIFUL VALENTINE

(Dedicated to Shami Jabane)

You are my beautiful Valentine, my love, my whole life, constantly on my mind.

When I am waiting for you, at an agreed meeting place, I shiver in anticipation of your arrival when I will, once again, see just how beautiful you are.

Just the sight of you, a word, a glance, a smile, is enough to move my heart into overdrive. Even a phone call out of the blue brightens my day. You have a magical touch.

You are my beautiful Valentine, an injection of life and love, and I am hopelessly in love with you, being swept along on an emotional, out of control tidal wave.

Cupid's arrow has penetrated deep into my heart. I failed to see it approaching and now it is stuck fast and cannot be removed.

Oh, my darling Valentine, please say there is room in your heart for me, or I will surely die from this wound.

I am so deeply in love with you that I would willingly, without a second thought, lay down my life for you.

This love will never disappear for it is too strong and overpowering, too deeply embedded in my soul.

Looking into your eyes takes me into another world, our world, where only you and I exist.

I love you, I love everything about you, my perfect woman, my true soul mate.

My impulsive, romantic gestures are all because of my love for you. I cannot think straight since being struck down by the arrow of love.

Rationality and common sense have been removed from my vocabulary and I am just following my heart.

Please say you will be my Valentine for, only then will this wound heal, only then will my heartache disappear.

My beautiful Valentine, my heart is overflowing with love for you . . .

Mark Pyne

ESTRANGEMENT

Green edges of
a fast fading, yellowing leaf
state
that
the spring the leaf has gone through
was very brief.
If only you knew
your absence is making me as well
a fast fading, yellowing leaf,
a vast expanse of ice
where evanescence is gliding down
on silent wings
blocking the echoes
of bygone springs.

Nayyer Ali

VALENTINE REVERIE

On Valentine's Day we'll walk in the woods
Where the bub'ling stream rushes down to the sea.
The clear spring sun shines through the high branches
Warming the daffodils waiting to burst and
Cover the ground in a carpet of gold.
Above us the birds are singing spring songs,
Sporting fine colours to impress their mates!
Do they know of love, or is it just us?
We two together enjoying our walk.
The touch of your hand sends warmth to my core.
A look in your eyes and I'm lost in your soul
Melted together as just one being.
All this costs nothing but is worth fortunes
Let's celebrate our love day after day!

Anne Lawry

UNTITLED

World in a spin
Spin I am in
Full of great expectations
Of love in the afternoon
Everybody loves a lover
Cooing and kissing
Valentine verse special feeling.

S M Thompson

THE OLD BOY

I never had the chance to know him.
He lives at the back of the mill, by the wheel that makes the river flow.
I think his name was Vern, plain,
Simple and pleasant, never caused much of a concern.
He lives at the back of the mill by the wheel that makes the river flow.
He was in the square picking the best flowers,
Giving each one a sniff facing the clouds,
Taking in the scented air, wandering back along the wharf.
Is happiness in his stride? Vern's the man caressed with life.
He spent many of his years mining Yorkshire's hills,
An industry now forged only in his memory.
In a pocket of a Yorkshire hamlet, he dwells on the vanished time.
He lives at the back of the mill by the wheel that makes the river flow.
Lives alone now, after the day she passed on,
Out spreading the crust along the yard.
It only seems like this morning she would still be there
Just as he remembered.
Watching the birds come close.
But they flew away with her soul.
My grandma.

Stewart Scott

FIRST LOVE

'You OK?' he whispered so sweetly in my ear.
'I'm fine,' I said, turning in his arms.
The first kiss, the first touch, the first love.

Rachel Ann Mills

FIRST LOVE

Dancing around freely with outstretched arms,
two seeds blowing gently across a golden field.
Synchronous in time, energies invisibly abound.
As the slow breeze settles, light tentative fingertips circle
towards the quickening burn of a guiding light.
Fresh spirits teasing the early morning spring . . .
warm scents, all of which intriguingly fragrant . . .
gently pushing together and through beaded nape,
the sweetness of nectar . . . breathing and moving,
rhythmically towards an everlasting yearning.
Worldly promises entwining and forever dancing
towards their awakening.

Carol Hunt

SAINT VALENTINE
(Dedicated to Trevor Wicks)

As our hearts entwine
I will compare you to my garden,
   Sweet Valentine
Clinging ivy
Gladioli
Tulips
Primrose
Lily of the valley
My rose of Sharon
Angel trumpet
And love in a mist
To name but a few
Yes, you are my knight in shining armour.

A love like ours
Would make a good television drama.

Christine M Wicks

EVERY DAY'S A VALENTINE

We do not need to find a date,
for, written in the sky above,
that day and every day besides:
I love, I love, I love, I love.

Now, Valentine and Proteus
two gentlemen of high renown,
both lost their hearts to maidens fair,
but only one would wear the crown.

We do not need to find a date,
for, written in the sky above,
that day and every day besides:
I love, I love, I love, I love.

Young Proteus broke many hearts,
for protean he was, in truth;
while Valentine, without such guile,
lost not the innocence of youth.

We do not need to find a date,
for, written in the sky above,
that day and every day besides:
I love, I love, I love, I love.

Which of the two as archetype
in my own case, you may divine:
not Proteus you'd have me use.
Please let me be your Valentine.

We do not need to find a date,
for, written in the sky above,
that day and every day besides:
I love, I love, I love, I love.

Adrian Brett

VALENTINE PAST ITS PRIME

She saw him,
He saw her.

She purred at him,
He purred at her.

She sidled over,
He slid to his side.

She said, 'Be my lover.'
He said, 'Be my guide.'

She took him to her place,
He thought luck was in.

She took off her face,
And opened the gin.

He took out his teeth,
Then lost his grin.

Her hair came off next,
He was getting perplexed.

She poured them a drink,
Then he started to think.

Should he go and take flight
Or just put out the light?

Sheila Bates

LOVE'S ETERNAL GIFT
(To Francine, my guiding star)

To me you are a summer's breeze caressing through my hair,
An autumn leaf of golden brown, drifting on the air,
A snowflake of such beauty, there is none who can compare.

I feel you in the morning with the first rays of the sun,
Your warm caress upon my skin until the day is done,
And as the night draws near and the moon comes out to bare,
I see you stood before me with the stars held in your hair.

I will never love another, the way that I love you,
When Cupid shot his arrow, I know his aim was true,
If I never see you from this day, my heart will not feel blue,
As I will treasure for all eternity the time I spent with you.

Paul Evans